GW00889976

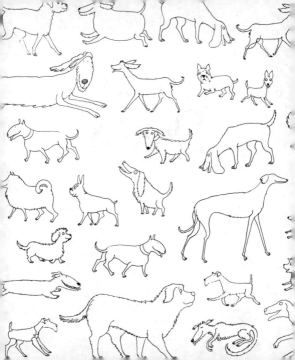

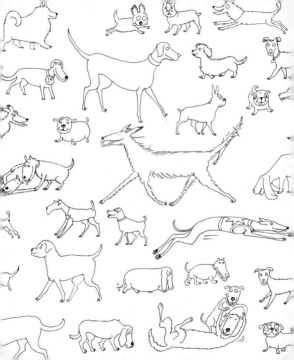

A Red Fox Book

Published by Random House Children's Books
20 Vauxhall Bridge Road, London SW1V 2SA

A division of The Random House Group Ltd
London Melbourne Sydney Auckland
Johannesburg and agencies throughout the world

3 5 7 9 10 8 6 4 2

First published in Great Britain by Red Fox 2000

Printed in China

THE RANDOM HOUSE GROUP Limited Reg. No. 954009
www.randomhouse.co.uk

ISBN 0 09 940872 4

# THE LITTLE
# BOOK OF
# DOGS

Judy Hindley and
Margaret Chamberlain

Wherever I go,
I look for dogs –
dogs are my
favourite things.

# BIG

dogs,

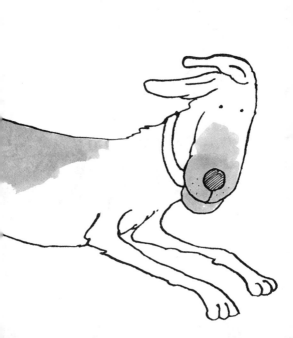

small

dogs,

# long
dogs,

**tall**

dogs,

any dogs,
all dogs.

Slick, neat,
show dogs,

very old slow dogs.

Dogs that work,

dogs that

*play,*

dogs that just sit
around all day.

Dogs that
waddle,

# dogs
that race,

dogs with
a little, flat,
squashed-up face.

Dogs with little pointy
ears that twitch
at every sound,

dogs with flippy-floppy
ears that almost
touch the ground.

A bulldog,

a beagle-dog,

a poodle-dog,

a pug,

a silly-billy

## sweet

dog,

a dog that's
like a rug.

Dogs in a shop,

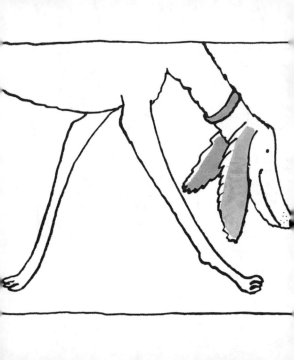

dogs in
a park,

dogs in a
house,

dogs in the dark.

# Dogs in a ring,

# dogs in a crowd,

dogs that are

gentle,

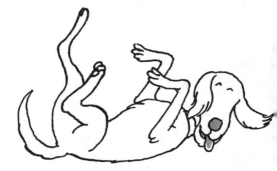

dogs that are

loud.

WOOF
WOOF

GGRRFF

larking
dogs,

# Walking dogs,

# talking

dogs.

White dogs,

brown dogs,

beach dogs,

# Clown
dogs.

Tall, slim,

# spotty

dogs,

snotty dogs,

grotty dogs,

goony, loony

crazy

dogs!

# Fat
dogs,

lazy
dogs,

freckled, speckled,
dotted
# dogs,

# knotted

dogs,

besotted dogs,

slim, lean,
spare dogs,

# HUGE

dogs,

square dogs,

hairy dogs,

scary dogs,

bouncy
*little*
merry
dogs.

Dogs that hunt,

dogs
that

*herd,*

# AMUSING
# DOG
# FACTS

Chanda-Leah, a toy
poodle from Ontario,
Canada, can play
the piano, count
and spell – five
hundred tricks
in all.

Chi Chi, a rare African sand dog, is officially the ugliest dog in the world. He's won the World Championship Ugly Dog Contest five times.

Black Labrador Iowa
has managed to sniff
out £1.45 billion
worth of drugs at
Miami airport.
Some nose!

The tallest
dog ever?
Great Dane
Shangret Damzas
from Milton
Keynes is 1.054m
(3ft 5½ in) high.

And the heaviest dog?
Aicama Zorba of La
Susa, a
mastiff
from
London
weighs
155.58 kg
(24st 7lbs).

# CHOOSING
# A DOG

Dogs have all kinds of
personalities. Take
some time to find the
one that's right for
your family.

Making friends with pet cats can be a little bit tricky...

And if you have a small house, don't let a dog choose you!

Not all dogs are good
with children. Toy
dogs aren't too keen
on noisy kids...

yip

strong dogs can be a
little unruly...

and big dogs will take
YOU for a walk...

Whatever kind of dog
you get, remember –
dogs are like family.
They'll want lots of hugs
and heaps of your time,
but they don't talk back!

# FEEDING
# YOUR DOG

One meal a day is all
your dog needs.

Doggy titbits are ever so
yummy; but a fat tummy
is what you will get!

Tasty chocolate treats
are a doggy no-no.
But dog biscuits
and chew toys
work a treat.

If your dog insists on lunching on grass, don't worry. A little salad is healthy for dogs too.

And for thirsty dogs,
don't forget fresh water
to keep their noses moist.

# GROOMING YOUR DOG

Dogs will run a mile at
the sight of the bath
towel, but baths are good
for dogs big and small.

Long walks keep your dog's
toenails nice and short,

but sometimes they may
need a trim at the vet's.

For shiny, healthy fur, brush your dog every day. If your dog has unruly, long hair, get it in style with a trip to the pooch parlour.

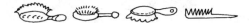

# TIME
# TO
# PLAY

Puppies especially love
to dig, run, and play
tug of war.

Take your dog out
and about and it will
soon learn how to
behave around other
dogs and people.

Tip number one: show
your dog who is boss.

# Tip number two: carry lots of doggy treats!

If you start early, you
can teach your
dog almost
anything:

sit and stay,

fetch, play dead,
roll over,

and give a paw.

# Dog
# Jokes

What did the cowboy say to his
dog when it fell off the cliff?
Dawg gone.

What do you get if you cross a
Rottweiler and a Lassie?
A dog that bites your leg off
and then runs for help.

My dog's got no nose.
How does he smell?
AWFUL!

What do trees and dogs
have in common?
BARK.

Postman: Your dog bit my ankle.
Dog owner: Well, he's only little – he can't reach your knee.

What dog keeps the best time?
A watchdog

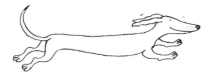

A hot dog goes into a bar and
asks for a drink. The barman
says, "Sorry, we don't serve
food here."

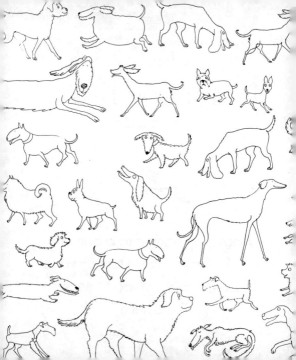